THE LANGUAGE OF
ANGELS

A Story About the Reinvention of Hebrew

Richard Michelson
Illustrated by Karla Gudeon

Charlesbridge

For Neil Waldman—R. M.

For Imogen, Stella, Rowan, Hannah, Henry & Tess: may the acquisition of words and language always be a happy, exciting experience for you!—K. G.

Special thanks to Rabbi Eliezer Ben-Yehuda, namesake and grandson of Eliezer in this story, for his encouragement and expertise.

Published by Charlesbridge
9 Galen Street, Watertown, MA 02472
(617) 926-0329 • www.charlesbridge.com

Illustrations done with watercolor, Pigma Micron pen,
    Jute handmade paper, and Photoshop
Display type set in Catalina Avalon by Kimmy Design
Text type set in Catalina Clemente by Kimmy Design
Printed and bound by 1010 Printing International Limited
    in Huizhou, Guangdong, China
Production supervision by Brian G. Walker
Designed by Whitney Leader-Picone

042134.4K2/B1040/A7

Library of Congress Cataloging-in-Publication Data
Michelson, Richard, author.
    The language of angels: a story about the reinvention of Hebrew / Richard Michelson; illustrated by Karla Gudeon.
        pages cm
    ISBN 978-1-58089-636-8 (reinforced for library use)
    ISBN 978-1-60734-896-2 (ebook)
    ISBN 978-1-60734-897-9 (ebook pdf)
1. Ben-Yehuda, Eliezer, 1858–1922—Juvenile literature.
2. Hebrew language—Revival—Juvenile literature.
I. Gudeon, Karla, illustrator. II. Title.
PJ4534.B4M53 2015
492.4092—dc23   2015026836

Printed in China
10 9 8 7 6 5 4 3 2

Once there was a child without a friend.

Two boys his age lived nearby, but they spoke Yiddish. In the morning they said "*guten tog*" to each other. Two girls down the road spoke Arabic. They said hello when they met. "*Marhaba!*"

Some children spoke Spanish. They said "*hola*" to their friends. Others spoke Ladino. They wished each other "*buenas tardes*" in the afternoon.

But Ben-Zion didn't speak Yiddish or Arabic, Spanish or Ladino. He didn't speak Turkish or Russian or English or any of the many languages spoken in Jerusalem in 1885. So he spent most of his time alone.

Ben-Zion's father, Eliezer, didn't want him to hear any language except Hebrew. Not even the language of animals. If horses were neighing or sheep were bleating or coyotes were howling or donkeys were braying, he covered Ben-Zion's ears. Really!

"You shall hear only Hebrew, the Language of Angels," he told his son. "You will be the first child in more than two thousand years who will grow up speaking only the beauty of our ancient tongue."

"A long time ago," Eliezer told Ben-Zion, "all Jewish people spoke Hebrew. They lived near Jerusalem in a kingdom they called the Holy Land. But there were wars, and their country was defeated. The people lost their homeland and moved to places all over the world. They continued to say the Hebrew prayers that their parents had prayed in the temple, but they learned to speak the language where they lived. Eventually they forgot how to speak Hebrew except for the words in prayers."

But Ben-Zion's mother, Devorah, was worried. Ben-Zion was already four. Sometimes he made sounds, but he never said words.

"Call me Mother. Say **Ima**," Devorah said. She pointed at Eliezer. "Say Father. Say **Abba**." Ben-Zion still said nothing. She wondered how Ben-Zion would ever find anyone to play with.

Eliezer didn't want Ben-Zion to be the only one to speak **Hebrew**. He wanted to start a school with all the lessons taught in the ancient language. He called a community meeting. Some men showed up to hear what Eliezer had to say.

"Lithuanian Jews cannot understand Jews from Spain or Turkey or America," Eliezer began. "My dream is to teach all Jews to speak Hebrew again. It's the language our prophets learned from God's angels."

A man named Zalman shouted at Eliezer. "But many of us speak Yiddish together! Hebrew is holy and should be used only for prayer. We should never use sacred words to talk about taking out the garbage or to ask for the bathroom."

"But we spoke Yiddish in the shtetls, when we were not free!" Eliezer yelled back. "The prophets did not speak only in the temple. Do you think they did not use the bathroom?"

"You must be *meshugge*," someone called out. Most everyone agreed that Eliezer was crazy.

When Eliezer returned home, he heard Devorah singing to Ben-Zion in her native Russian. He couldn't believe his ears. "I'm sorry," Devorah said. "Ben-Zion couldn't sleep, and I was trying to calm him with a song my mother sang to me."

Eliezer was furious. He yelled. He stamped his feet.

"Abba, don't be angry with Ima," Ben-Zion said quietly in Hebrew. His mother and father were silent. Then they both gave Ben-Zion a hug, and all three danced around the room.

Once Ben-Zion started speaking, he didn't stop. By the time he was seven, he spoke Hebrew as well as his parents.

But he still didn't have a friend he could talk to.

"Can I please have a dog?" he begged. "I want someone to talk with when you are busy."

His father agreed. "Now that you speak the Language of Angels,
I see no harm in hearing a dog bark."

Maher—"fast" in Hebrew—is what Ben-Zion called his best friend.
Ben-Zion tried to teach Maher Hebrew, but he wouldn't learn. He kept
licking Ben-Zion's face.

One day on a walk through the neighborhood, Ben-Zion and Maher
were followed by some big kids.

"Ben-Zion is speaking the Hebrew to his dog!" Zalman's son shouted.
"Papa says that it is wicked to talk the holy language to animals." He
threw stones at Maher, and other boys joined in.

Ben-Zion was in tears when he arrived home. He told Devorah that he'd never have a friend.

Devorah held him close. "Shush, my child. Don't blame those children. They learned to hate from their fathers, who are scared to learn new things. If only parents could learn from children, maybe they wouldn't be so frightened."

Eliezer listened in. If he wanted Hebrew spoken, he needed to teach children first and let them teach their parents.

One day Eliezer brought home ice cream. Ben-Zion wanted to ask for some, but there wasn't a Hebrew word. Because ice cream didn't exist two thousand years ago, no one in history had ever asked for it in Hebrew.

"We cannot just make up any word," Eliezer explained. "First we must see if there is a cousin in another language such as Arabic or Greek. Or maybe there is a similar word in Hebrew to describe a cold dessert. Words are related to one another. Making a new word is like solving a mystery or putting together a puzzle."

Eliezer looked through his books. He discovered the word *gelidus*—"ice-cold" in Latin. It reminded him of the old Hebrew word *glid*—"to freeze water." Eliezer had created his new word.

"Would you like some **glida**?" he asked Ben-Zion. But by then the *glida* had melted.

The next afternoon, the children in the neighborhood heard that Ben-Zion was sharing *glida* with anyone who asked for it in Hebrew.

"How will I remember the word *glida* the next time you have some?" one of the girls asked Eliezer. "Can you write down all the Hebrew words in a book so I can look them up if I forget?"

"I will write a book," Eliezer answered. But there wasn't a Hebrew word for "dictionary." Before Eliezer could write one, he needed a name for it.

Milah meant "word," and many place names ended with -on, so Eliezer invented the word **milon**. Now there was "a place for words" where Eliezer could record every Hebrew word, new and old. And everyone wanted to help make new ones.

Ben-Zion felt like maybe he might make a friend at last. Zalman's son joined in, though he didn't tell his father. He had an old bicycle, and he helped make up the word **offanayim** by combining the Hebrew word for "wheel"—**ofan**—and the ending meaning "a pair of"—**ayim**. He even let Ben-Zion take a ride.

Every word was a new adventure. The word for "book"—**sefer**—and "house of"—**bet**—were combined and became **bet ha-sefer**, Hebrew for "school."

"It is like building a school brick by brick," Eliezer said. "We are building a language word by word."

Children competed to make up new words, and Eliezer wrote them down in his *milon*. Just as Eliezer dreamed, children taught their parents. As years passed, teachers started teaching Hebrew at school.

בֵּית הַסֵּפֶר

And by the time Ben-Zion was grown, he had made lots and lots of friends.

עֵצִים
etsim · trees

שֶׁמֶשׁ
shemesh · sun

צִפּוֹר
tsipor · bird

פַּרְפָּרִים
parparim · butterflies

ḥaveri

AFTERWORD

The dialogue in the story is not translated directly from Ben-Zion's or Eliezer Ben-Yehuda's writings, but it follows the general framework as they, and history, have passed it down. In his autobiography, Ben-Zion described the strange measures taken by his father to ensure that he would hear and speak only Hebrew. He also wrote about his dog, Maher. The illustrations draw from folklore tradition and take some liberties for simplicity's sake. For instance, Eliezer and Devorah were following Sephardic Orthodox dress and customs when Ben-Zion was young, but they eventually returned to the more European look depicted here. The edible ice-cream cone wasn't invented until after Ben-Zion's childhood, but it did exist before Eliezer's *milon* was first published. And although Maher died as a puppy, we have given him a few more years with his best friend.

BEN-ZION

When Ben-Zion was seventeen, he traveled to France to attend university. He changed his name to Itamar Ben-Avi. Ben-Avi means "son of my father." He remained interested in words and language throughout his life. After college he moved home and became a journalist and publisher.

Itamar also wrote an autobiography and a biography of his father. Eliezer wanted all Jews to learn Hebrew so they could talk with one another, but Itamar wanted everyone in the world to be able to converse. He championed an international language called Esperanto, although it never became popular. He also thought that Hebrew should be written in Roman script, *abba* instead of אַבָּא, and Ben-Zion instead of בֶּן-צִיּוֹן.

ELIEZER

Eliezer spent the rest of his life working on his *milon*—the Hebrew dictionary. The first volume was published in 1908. After each Hebrew word he added

French, German, and English translations, and he included Arabic, Greek, Latin, Aramaic, and Assyrian references. He also explained the origin of each word.

When Eliezer first moved to Jerusalem in 1881, no one spoke Hebrew as their main language. But during his lifetime, fifty-five schools opened with all instruction in Hebrew. In 1948 the state of Israel was established, and Hebrew was made the national language. Today more than three million people speak Hebrew every day. Eliezer's dream did come true.

DEVORAH
Devorah Yonas Ben-Yehuda, the first mother in nearly two thousand years to address her child in the biblical language, died of tuberculosis when Ben-Zion was ten years old. She gave birth to five children, but only Ben-Zion and his sister Dola lived to adulthood.

THE HISTORY OF HEBREW
Hebrew began to die out as a daily spoken language around the time of the Maccabees, about 200 BCE. As Jews were driven from their homeland and settled in various parts of the world, they learned the language of their adopted country. Hebrew ceased to be spoken except in temple, and its vocabulary never increased.

When Eliezer Ben-Yehuda began working on his *milon*, there was no Hebrew word for any modern idea or object. To make up new words, Eliezer studied ancient languages related to Hebrew, such as Assyrian, Egyptian, Ethiopian, and Coptic. Arabic provided many words because it was the only Semitic language that had remained in use throughout the ages.

Biblical Hebrew didn't use vowels, but in Modern Hebrew, a system of dots and dashes has been added above and below the letters to make it easier to read and to indicate how words are pronounced. (Imagine reading English words without the vowels!) Hebrew is written and read from right to left, and books are printed "back to front."

PALESTINE

In 1881, Eliezer Ben-Yehuda immigrated to Jerusalem, the ancient capital of Israel. He considered himself a "Jerusalemite." At the time, the surrounding land was known as Palestine, and it was home to approximately 175,000 Palestinian Arabs, 25,000 Jews whose forefathers had remained in the area, and an assortment of people of other nationalities.

For more than four hundred years, the Holy Land was governed by the Turks. After World War I, British soldiers marched through the gates of Jerusalem, and Great Britain issued the Balfour Declaration. It proclaimed that Palestine was under English rule and was the homeland of the Hebrew people. The British governor of Jerusalem once even greeted Ben-Yehuda in Hebrew.

Soon there was fighting between Arabs and Jews to control the land, but Eliezer believed that Jews and Arabs were *mishpaḥa*— family—and should share the land and live together. He delivered a lecture at the Arabic Academy of Science about the close relationship between Arabic and Hebrew. He explained how he had borrowed many words from Arabic and that some Arabic words had been borrowed from Hebrew. Most Arabs respected Eliezer and were pleased to hear their "sister tongue" spoken in the markets.

FURTHER READING

Learn more about the history of Hebrew and the pioneers of its usage:

Ben-Yehuda, Eliezer. *A Dream Come True*. Translated by T. Muraoka. Boulder: Westview, 1993.

———. *Fulfillment of Prophecy: The Life Story of Eliezer Ben-Yehuda 1858–1922*. Charleston, SC: Booksurge, 2009.

Drucker, Malka. *Eliezer Ben-Yehuda: The Father of Modern Hebrew*. New York: Lodestar, 1987.

Stavans, Ilan. *Resurrecting Hebrew*. New York: Schocken, 2008.

St. John, Robert. *Tongue of the Prophets: The Life Story of Eliezer Ben Yehuda*. Garden City, NY: Doubleday, 1952. First published 1912 by Ulan Press.